The Big Beautiful

SABIHA AKHTAR

بسم الله

In the name of Allah

.

Author's Note

Allah knows, I have tried to write every line and every word from a place of goodness. Although some of the themes within them are harsh and some readers feel these themes might contradict the title of this book 'The Big Beautiful' – my intention is not to glorify depression.

Like many of you reading I, too, have struggled with love, heartbreak, grief, loss, depression, and numbness. But somehow as bittersweet as it is, Allah made it so all these heart-wrenching emotions make up the big beautiful He created. Without the times I've been forced to hand my loved ones over to the akhirah, I would have never known how to truly love the people that are still in my life. Having not said goodbye to the person I would have done anything to hold one last time, I now try my best to give my goodbyes as if Allah will take them the minute I leave the room.

Nevertheless, I know many readers might not feel ready to read poetry that may touch on grief, suicide, and depression – and that's okay. For now, you can put this book back on your bookshelf until you're ready to open it up and read what beautiful moments Allah has waiting for you. And they are waiting.

However, the Big Beautiful refers to a feeling that I continue to fail to describe. But I know every person reading this has felt it. That feeling you have when you wake up on Eid morning, or when you see the first snowfall as you look out your window on a winter night. It's the feeling you have when you see your mother smile, as she shows you all the baby pictures she took of you in the stack of albums she keeps in her cupboard. Or the tingling feeling in your stomach when you're sitting on your flight, waiting to take off to the other side of the world– knowing something promising is coming. And in the mess of the Big Beautiful there is death, heartbreak, grief, loss and I don't even want to type the rest.

My point is, this life is not meant for you and I, but Allah continues to show you these big beautiful things every now and then, so you stay here, just long enough to fall in love with Allah - so you can be within Him infinitely, in Jannat.

And I pray we see each other there.

Love,

Sabiha.

I pray these words hold you
when my arms can't

1.

before you go
let me tell Allah
of all the nights
you taught me to love Him

our story was not of one
that could ever touch the tale
of Khadija ﵂ and her Prophet ﷺ
nor did it follow the sweetness
of Adam ﵊ and Eve ﵍

but did our hearts and eyes
not eclipse into each other
like Fatima ﵂ and her Ali ﵊
before he gently lowered his beloved
into the dirt

let this be another hollow poem
that wafts back into the air
to become the dust particles
you wake up to
until Allah commands qadr
to finish off our love story
when we meet again
before the gates of Jannat

2.

Allah told me
to remind you
our Prophet ﷺ
stopped his entire army
so his beloved Aisha ؓ could find her necklace

now remind me
all the ways
your lover failed you

3.

I pray Allah does not take my soul
until I have shown you
all His pretty things

I will raise you
to notice His pretty signs
that perhaps the very breath you exhale
out of your lungs
is the exact air Allah blew into you
when He bought you to life

to notice the pretty nights
that you leave your bed and your lover
to talk to Him
of your injured days
are one of infinite moments
Allah smiles

I will teach you,
whilst this dunya takes your soul
you must wait
for Allah to show you
all His pretty things

so Allah will not ask you
on the Day of Judgement
*'so which of the favours of your Lord
would you deny?'*
Quran (55:61)

4.

we have seen Jannat
they have not

in sujood
I have walked with the winds of paradise
felt the waterfalls of al-Firdaus on my skin
tasted the sweet grapes of Eden
five times a day
we are with Allah

and they are not

5.

by Allah
the thread within your prayer rug
must tighten itself in sorrow for you

knowing it sits in the dust
in the lowest draw
of the lowest cupboard
in the hollow room of its owner
who has the lowest love for their Lord

6.

how the angels of Allah
must weep for you

do you hear the angels beg you
through the late hours of the night
to feel the presence of your Lord
when you open the Book of your Creator
just as Musa ﷺ felt
the same magnificence
when He split open the Red Sea

how Jibrael ﷺ must weep for you
as he watches the Bridge of Sirat
being tightened

7.

in truth
my body is tired
of carrying this heavy heart
but tonight, before Fajr
Allah might just order the angels
to carry it with me

8.

when Allah created these sound waves
He knew

our eyes would fixate
on the nearest star
dreading Israfil
to sound the trumpet

that the sweet echo of the adhan
would be His reminder
of how Bilal ☙ waited eagerly to recite
the call to prayer knowing
it bought comfort to the Prophet ﷺ

though we are not of the Sahaba
He knew the scream Aisha ☙ let out
that bought Medina to a halt
when the Prophet ﷺ took his last breath
as his body lay limp
on the lap of his lover

would still bring sorrow
through the Ummah
1400 years later

9.

I have only seen this Dunya
so I beg, at least one of you
tell me you have seen Jannat

tell me the waterfalls of al-Firdaus
are pouring into your coffins
pomegranates from the gardens
are falling into your palms
are the Sahaba still resting
from the battle of Badr

is Abu Bakr ﷺ planting olive trees
for the Prophet ﷺ to eat
is Fatima ﷺ sat underneath a palm tree
writing a love poem for her Ali ﷺ
is Bilal ﷺ still reciting the adhan
from the balcony of Asiya's ﷺ palace

tell me
when you walked through the gates of Jannat
did the angels smile at you
and finally say
'Peace be upon you
for what you patiently endured
and excellent is the final home.'
Quran (13:24)

10.

know that you, reader
and the wife of Firaun
might just have the same end
to your story

bittersweet was her death
to be stripped and tortured
in the midst of the desert
as she cried
oh Allah, build for me near You
a palace in paradise.
Quran (66:11)

so the skies were ordered to part
and her last sight would be Jannat's palace
but Allah never closed the skies
He left it open for you

so just as your Asiya ؑ did
look up to see the same moon
your Prophet ﷺ split in half

and take in the same stars
that gave Adam ؑ and Eve ؑ comfort
as the first beings on earth

the moons and the stars
are your palace
'Then will you not see?'
Quran (51:21)

11.

I still have my mornings with Allah
to wake with the sun beaming
directly onto my face
know He positioned the warmth
to be facing my windows
at an exact angle
measured by the most Kind
to wake me in the kindest of ways

how ungrateful I am
to ignore all the little ways
Allah tells me
I am Near
Quran (2:186)

He is near

12.

Allah made His promise
and whilst I wait
for the promise to come near

I pray when I die
angels will wrap my soul in their wings
and gently lift me
past the planes, clouds and moons
until I can finally hear
the call to prayer
by Bilal ﷜ himself

13.

Jibrael ﷺ
ask Allah
to forgive me
for telling Him
the story I should have lived

if I was granted everything I asked
my mother would be washing my body
the keepers shovelling my grave
this very night

14.

If Allah gave me one dua
would I ask the wife of Firaun
if I could rest
just one night
in the house He built for her
in Jannat

or in greed would I ask
Jibrael ﷺ to recite this very poem
to the Prophets
and Sahaba

in truth I would ask Allah
to take me away
for just a moment
and ask that He recite Surah Duha
directly to me

so I can hear Him tell me;
*'Your Lord has not forgotten you,
Nor is he displeased with you.'*
Quran (93:3)

15.

if Allah gave me just one day
would I rush to Medina
just to fall before the grave of my Prophet ﷺ
whilst hearing my final call to Maghreb

or like a fool would I run to my lover:
my comfort and my Jannat
and feel my terror dissipate
as I listen to him recite Surah Mulk
until my body is buried
to the same voice
reciting my Janazah prayer

in truth I would not make it to Medina
and my lover is no longer here
know that I would bow before my Lord
begging for mercy
for spending many nights in the dunya
trying to push forward my death
by my own impatient hands
without the permission of Allah

16.

did Allah not tell you
you have no knowledge of the unseen

yet you refuse to believe
the same angel that held the basket
of baby Musa ﷺ afloat
in the River Nile
before he was in the warmth
of the wife of Firaun

might just be the very angel
watching over your body
every night
when your soul is sharing its secrets
in the comfort of Allah

17.

In the name of Palestine
our Sahaba still live in the soil
of the planted olive trees
of Al-Aqsa

know, when the angel of death
kept the smallest coffins to himself
the Sahaba were in al-Firdaus
teaching Gaza's little souls
how they planted their olive trees
in the Old Palestine

while the Sahaba embrace our little children
and tell the stories of Al-Aqsa to these little graves
know that our olive trees will grow
until the Day the oppressors
are held accountable
for the grief
that hurt the Ummah

18.

what if Allah told you
the very water you use to make wudu
contains the exact droplets
from the river
that kept the Ark of Nuh ﷺ afloat

what if the angels cried out
trying to wake you for Fajr
knowing the wudu water
held droplets from the Red Sea
that was commanded to part
by the mere strike
of Musa's ﷺ staff

I am sorry
you limit Allah's love for you
to what you think of yourself
when the very water you use
morning and night
might just contain
little flickers of Musa ﷺ and Nuh ﷺ

19.

has Allah told you
of the love story He wrote
for His Khadija ﷺ

when Allah gently took Khadija's ﷺ soul
her Prophet ﷺ came across jewellery she once wore
falling to his knees
he held it close to his chest
terrified to let it go

with that same love
are you waiting for me
 at the gates of Jannat
just as Khadija ﷺ waited for her Prophet ﷺ

are you sat at the entrance of al-Firdaus
eager to introduce me to the Sahaba
that have spent mornings telling you
of the night their Prophet ﷺ
split the moon in half

have you asked Khadija ﷺ
if you can show me
the same jewellery her Prophet ﷺ held on to
after she passed

are you holding the door of Jannat open
waiting to hear my familiar footsteps
walking towards you

20.

upon this Eid Morning
the angels sigh with you
pushing the sun rays
towards your windows
waking you softly

perhaps the angels blow the scent
of your mother's food
wafting it gently with their wings
towards every corner of your home

to give you the familiar warmth
that the children of al-Firdaus
wait blissfully
for the mornings in Jannat
they can finally taste
your mother's fresh cooking

before the Eid Salah
know, the Sahaba above
have an empty seat
above the prettiest waterfall
just for you

and the angels hold tight
the door handles of Jannat
waiting for you to walk through
so they can witness the moment
Allah smiles at you

21.

you tell Allah you're waiting for Jannat
yet Jannat has come and never left

Jannat is knowing when the Prophet ﷺ wept
it was Khadija ؓ that held him and reminded him
Allah still loved him
it's knowing when Adam ؑ fell asleep in the heavens
Allah took a piece of his rib and created Eve ؑ
knowing even in Jannat
Adam needed Eve's love

Jannat is knowing our Prophet ﷺ would stay awake
crying for you
even as he spent his days being tortured
it is knowing after the Prophet ﷺ passed
Bilal ؓ wept and wept
until he could barely recite the adhan
Jannat is reading Allah loved Khadija ؓ so much
He told Jibrael
to give her His salaam

Jannat is reciting Surah Mulk
remembering when Allah said;
It is He who has created you
and endowed you with hearing (ears)
and seeing (eyes) and hearts,
little thanks you give. Quran (67:23)

Jannat has always been here
if only you knew

22.

Allah did not keep Jannat
to Himself

as you stand for Maghreb
do you feel the strands
from the fresh grass of Jannat
beneath your feet

in Sujood
feel the clear blue streams
of the River al-Kawthar
trickling passed your forehead
are your ankles soaked in the puddles
that the waterfalls behind Khadija's ؓ home
leave behind

when you stand for Zohar
the wife of Firaun
might just leave her palace door unlocked
so the whispers of your prayers
can comfort her through nightfall

know, Allah is beautiful
He brings the winds and scents
of al-Firdaus to you
five times a day
and you don't know it yet;
Jannat is already *here*
paradise is here

23.

by Allah
to walk to the mosques
on the wings of the angels
hearing the sweet adhan of Fajr

24.

if Allah gave you back to me
could I tell you all the ways
I fell in love with Allah

does Allah assign angels upon angels
to craft each snowflake with a chisel and hammer
until each flake has perfect symmetry
to dust them down to earth
just for us to tire of snow
to ignore these little miracles

know that
just for these snowflakes
to fall from the atmosphere
and settle upon your windows
all Allah needs to say is
Be, and it is.
Quran (36:82)

tell me
just as Allah gently placed
these snowflakes on my coat
did He just as gently
separate your soul from your body

25.

when your Prophet ﷺ split the moon in half
did the moon cower behind the nearest star
in fear it would not be made whole once again

so when your Lord splits your heart in two
why do you run to every sinful corner of this Dunya
to make you whole

why do the moons know of tawakkul
and you do not

26.

before Allah lifts your soul
take notes of what the moons are telling you:
Islam is here

the universe is expanding
so do the Rings of Saturn
the moons of Jupiter
and every supernova
drift further away from Earth
and inch closer to Jannat al-Firdaus
because they long to be close to Allah

and 10 years from now
when you are driving home with your beloved
you will turn to see your children
drifting fast asleep in your backseat
and as their eyes follow the moon outside their window
they will ask you in the purest of words
why the moon follows your car
and you will simply say
the moon is there to remind you;
He is with you
wherever you are
Quran (57:4)

you and your beloved
will both promise one another
your children will be raised to *know*
Allah will never leave them

so the Dunya will not teach them
in the same painful way
it taught you

27.

how mesmerised
the angels must have been
to have watched
star-struck
as Allah moulded you from clay

how little you know
of your Creator's instruction manual
perhaps you were created besides
the same Moons NASA fails to capture
the Moon beautified by every being
that exists in our Milky Way

I am sorry
the shaitans tell you
you were created besides the Firauns
when the very moon
the Sahaba fell in love with
and your Prophet ﷺ split in half
might just have been formed
the very night
He blew life into you

why don't you notice
your Lords magic
all around you

28.

upon your Nikah
know that I, your poet
pray you could have everything
I could not

the ink on your Nikah paper
mirrors the ink Allah signed in the book of Qadr
before the moons were spun into orbit
before your Prophet ﷺ ever laid eyes
on his Khadija ☾
even before He blew life into Adam ☾
when He wrote your lovers name beside yours

before your soul is placed gently
into the hands of the one
who shares your rib

will you not pray tahajjud upon tahajjud
that you and your beloved's marriage story
is the tale Fatima ☾ imagined
when she spent mornings writing her poetry
before her own love story even began

you will have everything
I could not

29.

did Fajr not tell you
she has been waiting for you

did Isha not comfort you
with the possibility
the angel that guards you in sujood
is the same angel that witnessed
the parting of the Red Sea
when Musa ﷵ hit his staff

as you rest your forehead for sujood
did Maghreb not remind you
when Medina fell into chaos
after the Prophet's ﷺ death
Abu bakr ﵁ could only collapse over his body
and kiss his forehead
as his final farewell

whilst you read this passage
understand the wisdom
behind Salah being given to the Prophet ﷺ
after his Khadija ﵂ passed away

30.

did my Prophet ﷺ adore the olive trees
because they love Allah
more than we do

perhaps the olive trees and lilies
spend their entire lives
growing towards the sky
trying to touch the lowest heavens
to be close to Allah

they continue to remember
when the Day of Resurrection comes
they will turn to dust

whilst we forget

31.

before you take
your first little baby steps in the Dunya
tell me
did Allah not design
the anatomy of your heart
before He breathed life into you

like your father
did He create you to be
the most radiant hafiza
will you see *the big beautiful* in the Dunya
through your father's eye
and wear his birthmark on your left cheek
as modestly as he did

did He organise the veins of your heart
to write like your mother
with piles upon piles
of love letters written to her Lord
stuffed under her pillow
will she too recite Surah Mulk
as lovely as her father did
after every quiet Isha

before my beloved whispers the adhan
into your fragile ears
know that Allah made His promise:
I am with you -
Hearing and Seeing
Qur'an (20:46)

so even when I am long gone
let this poem hold you
when my arms can't

32.

when Allah blew life into our forms
did we not fall in love with one another
in the realm of souls

just as the wife of Firaun
melted as she held baby Musa ﷺ
was her devotion not due to how Musa ﷺ held her
in the soulful world

tell me, reader
have you fallen in love with your Prophet ﷺ
because your soul knows
he might have held
every part of you in his heart
as Fatima ﷺ sat beside you
and wrote about your heart
in the realm of souls

how dear
you must have been
to the Prophets
before the Dunya seized
your will to live

33.

when Allah finished creating you and I
as He created our Prophet ﷺ and his Khadija ؓ
did He pause to look at the final design
and smile lovingly at our lifeless bodies

as Fatima ؓ and her Ali ؓ
were being moulded from clay
Allah knew Fatima ؓ would grow to fall for the poets
did He not paint literature into the heart of Ali ؓ
so Ali would spend his mornings
and nights in the Dunya
trying to captivate the heart of his beloved

moments before He blew life into you and I
He knew on the mornings His trials burnt the most
it would be your delicate recitation of every Surah
that would softly guide me through the heavy days
so He stitched together your melodic vocal chords
and tangled your heart, vein upon vein
until it spelt our daughter's name

even in Jannat I will wonder
did my soul gleam with the angels
when He chose to create me
from your rib

34.

when Fajr calls for you
does the thread of the prayer rug
ask Allah for permission
to wrap itself around your ankle
so you never leave sujood

perhaps the thread itself weeps
being the same strand
that was woven deep into the curtain
of the Prophet's ﷺ chamber
1400 years ago

did the thread witness
our Prophet's ﷺ mornings in Makkah
being tortured, humiliated
and the darkest hours of the night
begging Allah
to grant you Jannat in your grave

the thread
must tighten itself in sorrow for you
knowing it lays in the dust
in the lowest draw
of the lowest cupboard
in the hollow room of its owner
who has the lowest love for Allah

35.

Allah is beside you
this very moment

tell me why
your neck is turned
facing your shayatin

instead of the direction
of the One Who held you
as you took
your first little baby steps
when you came into the Dunya

36.

you have not seen the throne of Allah
the throne floats on infinite water
so what if

the rain drops that fall from the skies
are little spills that fell from the infinite sea
that sits below His throne
what if the sun was the smallest jewel
that fell off His throne
and landed safely in our Milky Way

could it be the stars
are trillions of little fixated screws
that are commanded to hold the throne
high above the heavens

know that His kursi extends
over the heavens and earth
and whilst your eyes would burst
upon seeing the majesty of His throne
know that it is here

your Lord is here

37.

such a lovely Nikah
you will have
all because this poet
prayed light-years of tahajjuds
that you will not have
the same love story
I did

it is your turn
to fall in love with a being
that holds the white gates
of al-Firdaus open
so the angels greet you first

for you to be the reason
he falls in love with Allah
staying awake every Fajr
telling his Creator
how grateful he is
to wake up to you
every lazy Sunday morning

you will write for each other
like Fatima عليه السلام and her Ali عليه السلام
and I will pray
it will never be your turn
to lose him
like I did

38.

If you knew this would be
your last Isha with me
that the angel of death
sat next to me
waiting for His command

would you lead the Salah
with the longest sujood
so Allah could take a little bit more time
mending me whole

after salaam, would you hold me close
just as Aisha ☙ held her Prophet ﷺ
would your body collapse like hers
when I am gently pushed to Al-Firdaus

and will you fall apart in sujood
and beg Allah
that I love you in Jannat
just as I loved you in the Dunya

will you recite Surah Duha
to comfort me with the same voice
that saved me from myself

39.

before you wake for Fajr
and see the sun rise from the East
what if Allah commands angels upon angels
to organise the clouds in the sky by size
as they praise their Lord
just for you
to ignore this little miracle of Allah

what if the clouds hovering above you
are the same clouds your Prophet ﷺ pierced through
on the Night of Miraj
when Jibrael ؑ showed him the heavens

when the angel of death takes me to my Lord
will he fly me to al-Firdaus
by gently placing my soul on the nearest cloud

before the clouds part
to show you the sun settling in the West
know, if Allah loved you less
perhaps He would not have commanded the angels
to hold still the cloud above you
before tonight's Isha
so the lightening would not take you
before your Sujood ends

40.

tonight, after isha
you will be left with the angels
that came down from al-Firdaus
and broke through the Earth's atmosphere
just to sit beside you

when the emptiness of the night settles in
know
the silence that overwhelms you
is the same silence that comforted Nuh ﷺ
when he spent night after night
building the Ark of the believers
at the peak of his isolation

it is the same silence
that echoed through Medina's night sky
as your Prophet ﷺ stood alone
reciting Surah al-Haqqah
before the Kaaba
and Umar ﷺ heard the words of Allah
for the first time
and fell in love with his Creator

know that the silence that is filled
with the whispering of the angels
holds you
just as it held Ali ﷺ
on the night his Fatima ﷺ left him
to be with Allah

41.

perhaps the Black Stone of the Kaaba
envies the moon above
reminding it of the white radiance
it once glimmered

tell me
as the Prophet ﷺ passed the moon
on the Night of Miraj
did the moon freeze in its orbit
to stare in awe
knowing it is merely a rock
hovering before the pure one
that once split it in half

how the moon must grow impatient
to glow above my window
knowing in hours' time
it will be in the night sky of Medina
as close as Allah would allow it
to glisten before the body of its Prophet ﷺ

are hailstones
the tears of the moon
as it cries over the very night
he saw his Prophet ﷺ fly pass
to the lowest heaven
1400 years ago

42.

It's 8 PM
you're praying Maghreb
your body is barely here
the dunya around you is loud
mothers hurry along
to drop children off to their Quran classes
the traffic outside causes havoc
it's loud here

ربنا لك الحمد
you fall into sujood
it's quiet
you hear the waterfalls of Al-Kawthar
and the sweet scent of Jannat is here
just as Allah described it
the distant laughter of Ali and his Fatima
echoes through Al-Firdaus
your mother plucks the mangos
from Adam's ﷺ fruit tree
and He is *here*
Allah is here

the car horns pull you back into the Dunya
and whilst your soul grabbed onto the fruit tree
to stop it from having to come back
you tell it
Isha will come soon
so He can remind you once more

Jannat is worth it all

43.

the Dunya and the Earth
are not alike

begin to write
your love letters to the Earth
for its kindness
in wrapping its surface gently
over the body of your Prophet ﷺ

for growing the grass that fell
from gardens of al-Firdaus
in the Amazon rainforest
are the Coral Seas little droplets
that trickled down
from the River al-Kawthar

how brave is Earth's skies
to preserve Allah's brush strokes
when He chose the colour palette
to create Earth with

know, beloved
Earth is the child of Jannat
and how pretty is the planet
to devote its surface
to hold you in Sujood

44.

has Allah not told you
your organs will speak for you
on the Day we stand behind the Sahaba

just as your Prophet's ﷺ lungs
will perhaps confess
Khadija ؓ was the air he breathed
and his eyes will chant
even the mumbles under her breath
bought the coolest sensations
on the most unsteady nights of Makkah

will your heart tell Allah
and every winged angel
standing before us
that it was you who asked the Sahaba
to leave their palace windows open
so every Fajr dua I prayed for you
could be heard
by every Prophet ﷺ
in al-Firdaus

will every nerve and organ
fall silent
because they know
my ribcage did everything
it anatomically could
to keep my heart from tearing
with every Fajr I prayed
without you standing
in front of me

45.

do the stars hear
the angels whisper tales
of how they fell in love
with their Creator

how child-like
the rings of Saturn must be
to push one another out of orbit
taking turns in being close
to the grave of their Prophet ﷺ
in Medina

might the angels be planting
lilies and sunflowers
within your graves
raising baby fish and corals
to swim in the rivers
of your coffins

how tired the angels are
of you underestimating
your Lord's magic

46.

and if Allah told you
the water to be used
for your Ghusl
has already been carried
out of the water wells

already bottled
collecting dust mites
in an empty corner of the Dunya
waiting for your soul to be lifted away
so the container can be popped open
and poured onto your lifeless body

would your last words be a lullaby
singing your longing
to stay in the dunya
or would you give your salaam
to the angel of death
and sigh gratefully
that it's finally time for you to see the One
you've been reading this love poetry about
after all this time

47.

as you are reading this
you are one word closer to the moment
the veil between you and your Lord
is lifted

you are now 20 seconds closer
to the moment your soul is placed gently
into the hands of the one
who shares your rib

and you are one poem closer
to the night you and your beloved
will sit in the gardens of al-Firdaus
near the palace of Asiya ﷻ
as Khadija ﷻ sits beside you
and tells you of the first moment
she ever laid eyes on her Prophet ﷺ

48.

are you yet to ask Allah
why you were created
from your beloved's rib
and not his heart

perhaps Adam ﷺ wondered too
why Allah softly took a piece of his rib
whilst he was fast asleep
in the comfort of al-Firdaus
to create his Eve's body

in the loveliest hours of Fajr
as you lay beside your beloved
know
it is *his* rib
Allah created you from
the rib that protects the heart
that sings every Ayah
of your Lord

a shame it is
you still don't know
your entire human anatomy
evolves around the love story
of Adam ﷺ and Eve ﷺ

49.

If I could
would I ask tawakkul
all over again
to bless me with the same mornings
that your Khadija ؓ
had with her Muhammad ﷺ

how I complain of sabr
after having prayed every tarawih
without you
knowing it was Allah that stayed
and wrapped my abaya around me gently
commanding almost every angel
to sit beside me in salah
and lift my dua to Him
on Laylat al-Qadr

If I could do it all over again
would I ask Qadr
to bring you back down into the Dunya
or would I let go of this greed
and let you sit by the Sahaba
witnessing the Prophet ﷺ
water his Khadija's ؓ prettiest tulips
in al-Firdaus

like you once did
for me

50.

to the callers of the adhan
by Allah

upon hearing the sweet adhan of Maghreb
know that Bilal ؓ echoes your words
from the edges of Jannat

I pray I follow your voices
to guide me across the bridge of As-Sirat
on the Day of Resurrection

until your adhan leads to the arms of my mother
as she sits beside the gate of Al-Firdaus
waiting for her daughter
to tell her
she passed the questioning
of Munkar and Nakir

51.

do you not feel Allah
all around you
when you bow before Him

when you rest your head in sujood
do you see the darkness
our Yunus ﷺ saw
when he was drenched in the whale's acid
and does the pain he felt
from the burning of his skin
pulse through you

when you bow
do you feel the crushing
your Prophet ﷺ felt on his back
as he was unable to stand from sujood
from the camel guts
the oppressors threw upon his back
do you feel the sorrow Fatima ﷺ felt
hearing the enemy laugh and sneer
until she lifted the bloody organs
off her father's body

if you truly know Allah
do you not feel the history of Islam
come to life all around you
when you prostrate before your Lord

52.

the day Allah takes my soul
just as Ali ؏ did for his Fatima ؏

hold my body close
and deliver my Janazah prayer

so your voice brings me comfort
one last time
before I am lowered into the graves
before my Judgement begins

53.

when you go back to Allah
tell Him I tried

before the sun rose from the West
and the stars they once worshipped
shoot down
onto your Mosques and Churches
even before Israfil
exhales into his trumpet

tell my Allah
I prayed Surah Mulk and His names
knowing His angels
were dying to listen
so they could fall in love with Him
all over again

tell Him I knew it wasn't enough
but I loved Him
with the last remains of my soul
the dunya let me keep

54.

to live a life in Jannat,

after Bilal ؓ leads the Maghreb Salah
with the same voice that comforted
the Prophet's ﷺ heart
could I be granted permission
to plant thousands of date trees
so I can gift it to the Sahaba

or instead could I plant the prettiest of tulips
and water them every Fajr and Asr
so the Prophet ﷺ could enter my garden
and pick Khadija's ؓ lilac tulips
to gift it to her every night

might I have the purest honour
of writing with the Great Arab poets
with Umar ؓ and his pen
hours and hours after sunrise
just to recite it to our Prophet ﷺ
every Maghreb

Allah knows this just might be
the most foolish piece ever written
but what I would do
to be the reason your Prophet ﷺ smiles
before breakfast
every morning
in Jannat

55.

perhaps the reason
why the stars shoot past our planet

is because they burst
in awe
after hearing the adhan
their Bilal ﷺ recites
every Maghreb
in al-Firdaus

56.

this search for Jannat
killed every logic
and sanity in my being

you might just find
letters upon letters
written to the coffin of Fatima ﷺ
asking the grave itself
if she heard the pleads of Ali
when he knew Munkar and Nakir
would soon take his place

or has the dunya
taken my sense so much so
that I would be seen frantically lifting
the cloth of the Kaaba
above and below
in desperate hope
that one of the times it is lifted
Allah reveals to me a gate of Jannat

like I said
this search for Jannat
killed every logic
and sanity in my being
but the Dunya cannot kill
what is already dead

57.

because of you
everything falls in love with Allah
just a little more

perhaps thousands of angels
descend to the lowest heaven
just to hear you pray
every Ayah of His Surah Qalam

might all the little leaves ask Allah
permission to drift off its branch
just for the winds to carry the leaf
over the loudest cities and softest fields
to finally land on your windowpane

just so it can hear
your voice whisper
the warm words of your Lord:
in the remembrance of Allah
do the hearts
find rest

Quran (13:28)

58.

before Jannat's current takes you in
and you raise our little children
before the morning runs tire you out
whilst their little school lunches
demand a fridge restock
before you teach them how to recite poetry
and their dinners use up all the garlic and ginger

will you write to me when our little ones
fall in love with Allah
will you whisper the adhan
in our daughter's little ear
just like we practiced
the morning after our Nikah

will you teach them the night dua
as you tuck them gently into bed
and when they ask you to read a bedtime story
will you take out this book
from the highest shelf
to read them their mother's poems
from these pages I wrote for them

59.

Allah leaves our bodies here
and takes our soul back to Him
when we sleep

my soul knows something I do not
what if every night
when I am with Allah
Khadija ؓ gives her salaam to my soul
shows me the moons of Al-Firdaus
as she whispers the poetry of Fatima ؓ

what if
every night
I've survived this long
because He shows me
the things worth staying alive for

60.

I like to think
when Allah blew life into me
He smiled
because He knew today
I would be writing love poetry
about that very moment

61.

I will tell you everything
Firaun did not know

he would begin sipping wine
from the finest vineyards of Egypt
to his lungs drenched
in the salty water of the Red Sea

whilst he once stood proud
on a balcony of gold and rubies
his heart satisfied
watching the young of Bani Israel
slaughtered bloody
under his command

he now knows
his wife, our Asiya ﷺ
glistens over her balcony
in the palace her Allah designed
seeing the same little children
Firaun turned bloody
feeding off the pomegranates of her gardens
sailing in the River al-Kawthar
with Adam ﷺ and Eve ﷺ

62.

will my coffin watch me
beg my Creator
to send me back to the Dunya
or will I sink into the gardens of my grave
waiting for my moment
to give my salaam
to your Prophet ﷺ

63.

Whilst you cannot whisper
even the smallest dua
to keep you sane and whole

what if everything you do not know
talks to Allah about you
before the sun rays come
to wake you each morning

what if every grain of soil
of the plants you water
begs Allah to be the chosen dirt
to fill your graves
so they, too
can feel the coolest rivers of Jannat
trickle into your coffins

might every cloud, every flower
every night sky, every heart
even the rustle of the leaves
ask Allah to keep you in the Dunya
so they can have another night
edging close to your bedroom window
to hear you pray another ayah of your Lord

so they can fall in love with Allah
just a little more

64.

and I knew Allah would stay
when I had already seen Jannat
on every iftar night of Ramadan
and every Eid sunrise
I prayed salah beside my mother

long before
her and I could walk through
the gates of al-Firdaus
as one

65.

I will not love Allah enough
until I know

the atoms that make up this Fajr air
might just be the same atoms
that pushed the waves of the River Nile
that carried the basket of baby Musa ☪
before he was in the gentle arms
of the wife of Firaun

until I believe the winds
that breeze past my curtains each morning
are perhaps the same winds
that sailed with the Ark of Nuh ☪
after 950 years of sabr:
begging the kuffar to love Allah
just as he did

know that the water vapour
that fill the clouds above me
might just be the same clouds
flocks of birds pierced through
against the attacks on the kaaba
by the King of Yemen
almost 1400 years ago

and I will not know Allah enough
until I fall into sujood
and feel every sun ray
every element and every atom
whispering the names of Allah with me
this very isha

66.

when Allah moulded your chest
did He pluck off the ripest fruit
from the tropical tree that sprouts
just below His Kursi
in al-Firdaus

and did He command the fruit to pump
to attach chambers and veins
on each side of its fruit peel

just before He breathed life into you
did he softly place it into your chest
to name it the heart

I loved Allah
because I lived my trials with you

67.

before the mosques close after isha
and the prayer mats are folded away
before the night duas are whispered
and the bed sheets are dusted

could you ask the moons
to read you the night
your Prophet ﷺ lay fast asleep
in the Cave of al-Thawr
beneath the stars

did the cave witness
the insect edge towards your Prophet ﷺ
only for it to be written
that the insect tear apart
the foot of Abu Bakr ؓ
so his Prophet ﷺ slept untouched
to stay dreaming
just a few minutes longer

after this poem
will you not hear the quiet cries
of Abu Bakr ؓ echo through your nights
whilst the angels sit by your beds
rushing you to remember
these love stories
written by your Lord

68.

It's you
that Allah chose
to polish the Dunya off my body
and remind me
of the fresh spritz of Jannat

and now
I beg
you're dusting the curtains in our palace
and growing the finest sunflowers
you'd always buy me
with our Sunday breakfast

in al-Firdaus
waiting for me
to come home

69.

if Allah told you then
what you know now
would you still ask your Creator
to send you back to the Dunya

little sorrow you have
for those tragic minutes
sabr watched
your Prophet Nuh's ﷺ heart crack
by the order of Allah
as his lover and son
refused to board the ark:
to drown before his eyes

how you refuse
to give your heart to your Lord
when Nuh ﷺ walked through the gates of Jannat
knowing his beloveds
would never touch these gushing rivers
or feel the cooling embrace of their Prophet ﷺ

like the son of Nuh ﷺ
you and I know nothing
of فِي سَبِيلِ ٱللَّهِ

70.

the morning His oxygen
floated into my lungs
Allah might just have commanded
little pieces of Jannat
to stay with me

might the breakfast
Allah created just for me
be cooked with the pomegranates and grapes
that grew from the seeds
that had fallen long ago
from the Gardens of al-Firdaus

the raindrops that fall through the atmosphere
that grow our lemon and orange trees
might just be the tears angels shed
when they witness
the kindness of Allah

how much longing these tears must hold
wanting to return to the skies
and be close to their Creator
once again

when I am finally buried
into the soil that has been written for me
will I take these pieces of Jannat with me
to hang these grapes back on the branch it belongs to
and return these raindrops to the angels they fell from

how long Jannat has been carrying me
since I took my first little baby steps
in the Dunya

71.

when you wake
for tomorrow's tahajjud
come closer to al-Firdaus
and you just might hear it say:

as you fall into sujood
in the next few minutes
every cloud, every strike of lightening
every angel, every Sahaba
the plants and the planets
will fall into sujood
with you
in this simple Fajr

and know
you will never be more alive
and human
than you will be
in the next sujood to come
and the one after that
the one after that
and the one
after
that

72.

and Fajr asks me
once again

if Allah were to tell you
the dunya had been kind to you
that you will never touch the moons of Jannat
were He to command the angels
to seal shut the gates of al-Firdaus
and place thousands of miles
between your soul and the Sahaba

were the wife of Firuan
to lock her palace doors
and make dua for Allah to lower you
to the fire of the forgotten Firauns

were the angels to approach you
with a nail and hammer
to screw down the sacred veil
between you and your Lord
so it would never be lifted

would you still turn away
from the loveliest Surahs of your Lord
and live through the ayah
of Surah at-Tawbah:
they have forgotten Allah
so He has forgotten them
Quran (9:67)

73.

when your Prophet ﷺ lived
the loveliest of lives
did he not come here to say
your Lord is closest to you
in sujood

as your skin falls into your prayer mat
might every organ and cell
push through your skeletal system
so they too
can be this close to their Creator

when your blood rushes to your fingertips
and your bones slightly collapse over one another
when your skin sinks further into the ground
to hear you whisper
سُبْحَانَ رَبِّيَ الأَعْلَى

they know in this sujood
the Sahaba were just here
in the Battle of Badr
that today 70,000 angels are too
falling before Him in another Kaaba
that sits below His throne
in the seventh paradise:
Bait-ul-Ma'mur

all prostrating with you
in this radiant Maghreb sunset
between you and your Allah

74.

all these pretty mornings
Allah wrote for me

hear the cars pulling out of their driveway
to pray their usual quiet Fajr salah
perhaps the sun itself is being lifted
by the angels and Milky Way
upon the command of Allah

what if the stars are gleaming, excited
as sixty thousand angels
silently tuck them away
so they can finally reflect their nur
on the grave of their Prophet ﷺ
in Medina

are doves migrating from Makkah
tweeting and singing
their usual fajr dhikr
after having spent their nights
gliding above the graves
of their Sahaba

light-years it must take
for you to accept
'He is with you,
wherever you are.'
Qur'an (57:4)

75.

how lovely is Allah
to design my soul
and mould my clay
with the past forms of my mother

so her bodily features
and little memories
stay with me
even when the soil of the graves
wrap their arms around her body
and she is finally carried above
to her Allah

76.

before the market men of Morocco
dust their rugs
and the cats of Istanbul
take their first yawn of the day
before the date trees of Arabia
drop their ripest dates of the season

can I go back to the time
my Lord created the Universe
to a time before Adam ﷺ and Eve ﷺ
ever fell in love

just so I can see
even if it's for a fleeting moment
how He stacked the heavens
one above the other
perhaps He rolled the planets out of His hand
into the galaxy
so it could spin in a timed orbit

creation, itself
is poetry

77.

the spaces of the graves are filling up
how long these queues are
of beings lining up
to meet their Creator

and before I meet
Munkar and Nakir
in the junction between
the Dunya and Jannat

just as Allah wrote
for these dandelions
to find their way back
to one another
even after the winds blow them
over oceans and palaces

I made dua
Allah had written
to move my grave
just beside yours

so even in death
I stand before Allah
and give my salaam to the angels
with you next to me

78.

when Allah moulded these little fingers
from the most delicate of clays

did He mirror the fingerprint of Adam ﷺ
and carve the same little swirls
on your fingertips
just so you could fill
the hollow wells in the Dunya
with Adam's ﷺ devotion and purity

in my dreams and duas
I raise you
to settle into this life
with the same modesty of Fatima ﵂
and the gentleness of Abu Bakr ﵁

you will become everything
I could not

79.

when your Prophet ﷺ spoke
little by little
did every being in the seventh heaven
descend to the lowest galaxy
just to hear him give his morning salaam
to his beloved Khadija ؆

or did the seas
that wash over the pearl palaces
in Al-Firdaus
trickle passed Musa ؆ and Adam ؆
and touch the clouds
to be the chosen raindrops
that fall onto Earth
and soak through the Prophet's ﷺ cloak

did they ask Allah
permission to give up Jannat
for a fleeting moment
just to peek through the clouds
and see the Prophet ﷺ
bury six of his children

80.

how silent your heart was beating
when I lowered your small coffin
after you returned to Allah

whilst I couldn't do ghusl
to the body that was not in my arms
my Creator ordered the softest of angels
to pour the clearest of blue waters
over your little hands and feet

and perhaps whilst I sat listening
to the imam recite the dua of your Janazah
the angels were knitting a blanket
lighter than the one I made for you
so your grave would be soft and fresh
to hold you
until it's my turn to settle
into the grave next to yours

81.

when Allah ordered the whale to swallow
one of the loveliest of Prophets
were the seas in awe of their Creator
for being commanded
to guard the akhirah of the Prophet ﷺ
that almost gave up on his Lord

and does the whale cherish
the part in its body
Yunus ؑ fell into sujood
and cried out
'Truly I have been
one of the wrongdoers'
Quran (21:87)

today
does the whale still flow with the waves
along the shores
of the Atlantic or Arctic
or Pacific Ocean
knowing any day now
Allah will order
His coming command
and it will turn
to dust

82.

this piece I write
might be the nearest I will ever be
to Makkah
so tell me
all that you know

when you first laid eyes on Makkah
did you feel the memory of Umar ﷺ
hiding behind the cloth of the Kaaba
the night he listened to the Prophet ﷺ
pray Surah Haqqah
the night he fell in love
with his Lord

when you sighed to the skies
and saw the birds glide below His clouds
did your heart flinch to the memory
of the thousands of birds that attacked
the King of Yemen
when the Kaaba stood under threat

when you left Jeddah Airport
and took those first steps
off the plane
did you praise Allah
because you knew soon
you would be walking with the Sahaba
towards the house of your Lord

83.

when the Hour comes
and Allah commands the stars to fall
just as icicles fall
on a sharp winter night

the moment the sun
releases its hydrogen gas
to have it decay our Milky Way
seconds by seconds
death by death
will not nearly hurt me

or the instant two angels
we all know too well
sit beside my coffin
and ask me three questions I know to come
I pray I won't flinch

but to have my Lord turn away
when I stand before Him
on the plane of Arafat
and tell me
I was His dearest disappointment

now that is a poem
I never wish to finish

84.

light-years before
Allah wrapped the rings around Saturn
and the stars were commanded to glisten

centuries prior to these graves filled
with the ones I loved
before these trees ever fell into sujood
even before your Prophet ﷺ ever stood
before the crisp splitting of the moon

Allah chose my name
and my heart
and He wrote it within
the early chapters of my tale
but the most bittersweet chapter
He ever wrote for me

were the pages that said
you would be sitting
next to the prettiest gate of Jannat
waiting to tell me all about
the Prophets and Sahaba you met
after you left me
In the Dunya

85.

do the stars draw the night sky's curtains
so the sun and the moon
take turns being alone with Allah

how quickly the night
dissolves into the day
what if the suns and moons
sorely tell Allah
of all the cracked sinners
they've seen in the Dunya

but perhaps they mention you
by name
to the Most High

how the sun might tell Allah
it fell in love with you
that Tuesday morning
you thanked Him for the sun rays
that kept the graves warm
and caused their lilies to grow

what if the moon tells Allah
you left behind your beloved
to stand beneath His moon and stars
just so you could cry your dua to the One
Who waits for You in the lowest heaven
every night

and perhaps they ask Allah
to be the chosen ones
that look after your grave
when you've returned to the soil

86.

my duas could never measure
to the ibadah of the angels
even if I gathered all the clouds
and reshaped their water vapour
to spell out the Ayahs He wrote

even if I could peel
the first layer of the Earth's crust
and cover the graves of Medina
to shelter them
from the harshest winds of Arabia

how little is my dhikr
compared to His angels
even as I write this poem
the angels copy these words into their books
whilst they sit on my shoulder

and how fast this book will disintegrate
when the Hour comes

whilst my book of deeds
signed off
by the authors on my shoulder
will last
infinitely

87.

you can't sell your soul
to the Dunya

when He knows the reason
you fall into sujood
these tired mornings and nights
is because you hope
that one of these times
that you bow

you'll no longer be staring
into the tired threads
of your prayer mat

you beg that this time
you'll open your eyes
and you might just see
the moons of Jannat
telling you
you're home

88.

before the Hour comes
and the angels no longer
lift my praises to Allah

let every word of Shakespeare
every letter of Jane Austen
dissolve from their pages

and may the Dunya know
of the greatest love story
every written
the Bittersweet tale
of how a sinful poet
fell in love with her Lord,
the Most Kind

89.

before Allah keeps you to Himself
let the Dunya stand still
so I can write you the dua
I prayed just for you

I've asked Allah
to keep the most radiant of fireflies
hover over your grave
so I don't leave you
to the angels in darkness

that I asked Allah
to blow the sweetest of winds
to keep your gravestone weightless
and make room for the freshest drops
from the River al-Kawthar
to hydrate your grave

even in death
I pray my tawakkul is enough
to soften your akhirah

90.

you should know
I already made the heaviest of duas
to your Creator

when I asked Him
to loosen the bolts of your coffin
so the gentle breeze of al-Firdaus
and the sweetest grapes
from the gardens off the Sahaba
fall into your grave

91.

before the oceans no longer exist
and these glowing cities turn to dust

I ask You, Allah
to not let me go
until You've shown me
all Your pretty things

how pure the seas must have been
to spit out the drowned body of Firuan
how devoted the oceans were to You
to waft the whale of Yunus ﷺ
below to the deepest of waters
just so it could hear him
fall into sujood

and
the prettiest thing of all
my mother who bows with me
through every sunrise till sunset
might have been loved
just enough
to have the exact fingerprint
that Allah created
for Adam ﷺ

who am I to limit Allah's love
when He invented the words
Be, and it is.
Quran (38:82)

92.

even if I could tear the Dunya apart
brick by brick
grave by grave

even if I could peel off
every concrete pavement
and open every dust mite
that wafts through the corners of the Earth

I would still
never be able to find
the heart I once lost to the Dunya

93.

when Allah painted the Earth and the Heavens
did He dust the colours of the sky
with faded orange, rose blue
and every luminous shade of mauve
to match the colours of His Throne

and are the cloud's vapours
formed from the breath of the angels
or are they created from the ice crystals
that fell from the River al-Kawthar

are the flowers that grow
outside my window
every spring
the same flowers my Prophet ﷺ gifts Khadija ﵂
after every Fajr sunrise
in Jannat

how can I ask Allah
to take back my body and soul
when I am yet to remind all of you
all the beautiful things
He made just for you

94.

when the Jummah sun rises
and the sun pierces
its soft rays
through my curtains

I know
it's the suns shift
to remind me of His Warmth
on the moons behalf

and one day
I will draw the curtains open
for the last time
and the sun will no longer
remind me of Allah

in the background
news channels will murmur
through bewildered reporters
"The Sun has risen from the West."

and from that day on
'eyes will stare in horror'
<small>Qur'an (14:42)</small>

95.

did the coffin of Fatima ؏
crack
when it felt her Ali ؏
collapse outside her grave

and did she hesitate to walk through
the gates of al-Firdaus
as the poems he wrote
and his cries at her death
stayed with her

how sore Ali's ؏ soul must have been
to lose his Prophet ﷺ
and his beloved
to the akhirah
one
by one

96.

how the stories of the Quran
run through the anatomy
of every huffaz

perhaps the poetic nature
of the wife of Firaun
is the same love Allah used
to mould your heart
and attach the arteries

how every whisper of Yunus ﷵ
and repenting wail he cried
in deepest of oceans
pushes through every cell
of your blood stream

or perhaps the genius of Nuh ﷵ
sits in every crevice of your brain
the same logic he and the angels used
as he shaped and hammered
the ark of the believers

how poetic your being must be
to carry the beauty of Yusuf ﷵ
through your words and souls

know that the huffaz
bought the Quran to life
in every organ
because they know, any day now
the Ayahs of the Quran
will vanish from their pages

97.

it is Ibadah to wonder
how Allah's Creation works

are the millions or billions
of angels He created
divided into infinite sections
beneath His Throne

and are they worshiping Allah
in endless factories
currently following the command of Allah
designing the floorplan
of the palace you will abide in

and are they mirroring the blueprint
Allah built
for the wife of Firaun
when she was stripped and tortured
just for loving Allah

for Allah to carve
all these little lines
into my fingers
and give life
to my own unique fingerprint

for Allah to assign a billion more angels
to keep this planet
in its orbit

all He has to say is
'Be, and it is.'
Quran (38:82)

98.

there is a shoemaker
that works tirelessly
through years of hot summers
working in the lowest basements
of the Middle East

and when he stitches through
the rims of your soles
does he not feel
Fatima ☙ sewing through
the bloody cuts of her Prophet ☙
pulsating through his hand

does the thread remind him
of the time Fatima ☙ stood before her father
blotting away his blood
all because he told his people
Allah would hold them
if only they believed

how the quietest of people
that you walk by in every tall city

and silent mosque
are the ones that know
in the remembrance of Allah
do the hearts find rest
Quran (13:28)

the hearts
find rest

99.

pen and paper were given to me
as a Mercy from my Lord

and as I'm writing
these final lines
I pray Allah is guiding my pen
to write words
that will intercede for me
on the Day of Judgement

100.

how you sell your heart to the Dunya
as if Allah didn't mould it from clay

and how you wish to undo the clay
Allah put aside
to create your skin and bones
and every vessel of your heart
to show every shaitan of the Dunya
your form
is His most loved sculpture

how less you are
for regretting your being
when the only fact
Allah wanted you to know
after all this time

you are
and will always be
the most beautiful of creations
He chose
to breathe His life into

101.

when you talk to Allah
the angels sitting on your shoulders
will scribble down
every dialogue of your heart

so when the night falls
and your body cracks on your prayer mat
will your duas be so sincere
that they take the angels back
to the old towns of Mesopotamia
where Nuh ﷺ was left alone
with his hammer and chisel
to build the ark
as he cried to His Allah
just like you

or when you talk to the one
who holds the other half of your rib
do the angels sense the same gentleness
Eve ﷺ had
when she spoke to her Adam ﷺ

what if on that Day
the angels bow before Allah
and say they were grateful
they were ordered to sit in your shoulders
because through every loud trial
you survived in the Dunya
you took them back to the years
they sat on the shoulders
of Adam ﷺ and Nuh ﷺ

102.

the Mosques of Istanbul
waft the scents of Jannat
to remind me
I'm almost home

and just before
the gates of the Mosques are locked
and the doors are sealed shut
before the fitnah of the Dunya
dim the light bulbs
and slowly seeps its way up
the walls of the prayer rooms

can I hear
the imam of Hagia Sofia
or Sulaymaniyah
or even the Blue Mosque
recite their adhan
so the hearts find rest
for a final time in the Dunya
before the gates of Jannat
are released

before
I'm home

103.

and when I stand for isha
or fajr or zuhr
or maghreb or asr
I feel Allah
wiping the cold streets of the Dunya
away from my skin

and maybe
just maybe
Allah let's a little sun ray
from the stars of Jannat
to glisten onto my prayer mat

to remind me
He is *here*

104.

before Allah sent you here
did He order the angels to gather
and diligently weave
the thread of your prayer mat

and did thousands of the angels
wait with sabr
for the day you rolled out
that same prayer mat
and fall into your first sujood

and are they waiting with you
right this moment
for you to pray the next salah
so they can stand before Him
with you

you
and a billion other creations
are waiting
for the next adhan
to be called

105.

a passage from a letter I wrote to Allah
sometime in May

'...I have loved hard and lost even harder.
But when all is said and done,
when the bodies are buried, and the doors are closed.
When the immediate grieving season has passed,
your heart which was once sealed shut with the janazah
adhan,
finally unravels itself
and leaves a little crack exposed for warmth to come in.
The dread of grief subsides a little
and you let your loved ones waltz back into your heart and
soul.
Let it be heard from here to the heavens;
the only one I pray I never lose love for
is You, Allah.

I am blessed I have You,
I am grateful I have had You,
And I pray I will always have You.

just as my Prophet ﷺ said
The pen has been lifted
and the ink has dried.'

106.

the first moment
I was ever swept away in love
after Allah
was with you

maybe it was every little dua you whispered
after you would wake for Fajr
or was it the grace of a thousand angels
you carried in your voice
when you spoke of Allah

how your recitation of Surah Duha
settled down the heavy nights
and repainted my mornings
in the most vibrant of colours

and
although you're no longer here
the way you loved Allah
will hold me
the rest of my days in the Dunya

and now
after all this time
I've let you go
to follow the Qadr
your Allah wrote for you

107.

how uncomfortable it is
to wear the Dunya on your skin
just like this

like a damp sleeve
that just won't dry
after wudu

yet
unsettled in the Dunya
you are willing to stay
like a relentless itch
under your skin

until Allah commands
the flowing waterfalls of al-Firdaus
to rinse the Dunya off the chests

and dry off in the warmth
of the thousand moon rays
in the Jannat He created
just for you

108.

the grave sung your name
so you followed its voice
into the soil

how long I must wait
for the heavens to summon me
so I can rush after you
and come home

CHAPTER
109

"Didn't you ask for this?" said Qadr.

110.

just as I put on these fresh sheets
and dust my bed
after every fajr and isha

perhaps Allah
has commanded the maker
to install white sheets into my coffin
or is the tree bark
used as the wood for my coffin
currently being carved

and finally
after all this time
rather than my soul
returning to Allah
for a few hours during night fall

I beg
when it is time
I will be tucked lightly
into the grave Allah made
just for me
in the glistening gardens of Jannat
so I can tell Allah
I loved Him
for the story that I lived

111.

I am not sahaba
but even I feel
the heart tugging at its arteries
my rib cage cracking through my skin

when I hear of
the death of my Prophet ﷺ

the one Prophet ﷺ
who cried to the stars of Medina
to save the ummah
to save
me

112.

I can never wash the Dunya
off my skin

even if
I spent every late hour
of the next 70 years
retracing the steps of Musa ﷺ
gathering every droplet
of the Red Sea

113.

the voice of the adhan
whispers the sounds of Jannat
from every mosque
that sits quiet in the Dunya

and soon you will hear
sounds that will make you whole
from the near laughter
of Adam ﷺ and Eve ﷺ
echoing through each Jannat

to the sound of Umar ﷺ
rewriting and scribbling
the notes of his own precious poetry

and when that morning comes
that you hear the light and cosy conversation
of Khadija ﷺ and Fatima ﷺ quiet down
and Bilal ﷺ recite
the most beautiful adhan that was ever called
you won't remember that violin or piano
that once bought you to your knees

so before you are deserving
of hearing the voice of your Lord
fall in love with every delicate sound
Allah made for you
beginning with

حي على الفلاح
hasten to Success
حي على الصلاة
hasten to Prayer

114.

how long you took
to read your Quran
and fall in love
with the ones
who came before you

115.

what will happen to Jannat
on that Day

will the forbidden tree
let out the screams it held back
since Adam ﷺ and Eve ﷺ ate from its fruit

and might Safa and Marwa
grow as magnificent as ever
trying to hold the seven heavens
from falling through His Milky Way

will every waterfall
drown the arrogant
like the Red Sea
took Firaun

on that Day will the women of paradise
use every inch of their bodies
to shut the gates of Jannat
trying to be exempt from facing
the promise of Allah

will every pen on Earth
obey a command of Allah
and start writing

the Ayah of Surah Al-Qamar:
'The Hour has come near,
and the moon has split [in two]'

Qur'an (54:1)

116.

but fajr is different to the others
the morning air stays crisp
as if Earth was created last month

and whilst the stars
are being shooed away
for that fresh second
I fall into sujood
everything is still
so still
that I'm sure the Earth slowed its orbit to a halt

and as soon as I stand
from that one sujood
the earth resumes its orbit
and the air turns humid once again

but I have tomorrows tahajjud
for Allah to descend to the lowest heaven
so He can remind me
He's here

and I can have another morning
to fall in love with Him
all over again

117.

by the kindness of my Lord
I will wake to the dunya every morning
and I will live
for Him

so when it's my turn
to settle into the soil
I never utter the words

my Lord
send me back to the dunya

118.

do the dunya and the akhirah
share tales with one another

did the dunya weep
when the time came to pass
its loveliest of Prophets ﷺ
over to the akhirah

did it hurt the Earth
so much so
the seas became a little drier
and the clouds became a little greyer

and did the akhirah
vow to meet the dunya every night
to tell it of all the mornings
the Prophet ﷺ wakes besides Khadija ﷺ
and all the evenings he sits
and laughs through
with Fatima ﷺ

to remind the dunya of the Prophet ﷺ
that once lived
on its soil

119.

for all those
who gave their hearts to the dunya
before they gave it to Allah

does Allah not wait for you
in the lowest heaven
on all 365 starry nights
of the year

perhaps the angels hold their breath
waiting for you to grab your shovel
and unbury the heart
you once gifted to the dunya

and tonight
will you not throw the heart
high up to the skies
just for Allah to capture it
and mould it whole
with the same clay He used
to create you
billions of years ago

120.

the morning
Allah kept you to Himself
every vocal cord and sound
was lowered into the graves
with your body

until my duas
could no longer be whispered
only written
amongst these poems

until sabr
was all I knew

121.

but by Allah
I will write and write
until these little poems
will speak for me
on the Day of Judgement

122.

The blueprint belongs to Allah.

From the warm evenings I stuttered through my first Surah Fatiha, to the father that was chosen to whisper the adhan in my ear. From the mother's fingers that I wrapped my little hands around for the first time, to the first oxygen atoms that would float into my lungs. From the baby crib that I slept in at my new home, to the first Quran class my mother dropped me off to, at the end of my road. From my first fast of Ramadan, to the fifth time I just *couldn't* recite Surah Baqarah. The blueprint that led to that fleeting March when I laid my eyes on you for the first time, to the ink that was chosen to sign my name besides yours. And last, from the Janazah I buried my first body, to this last page I wrote in my first book.

Yet I worry when the blueprint was signed off
 by the Greatest Writer
 of all time:
Allah.

فى أمن الله
I leave you in the care of Allah

Acknowledgements

Allah.

my whole heart: amal, amaya & azlan/zazu
for cuddling up to me when I needed them the most.

mum, for bringing me my morning chocolate croissant from
lidl and dad (and one of my favourite people) for being so
wonderfully odd & shaving his eyebrows off for no valid
reason.

infinite love for zoya & sama & aisha & fariha & yaseen &
zaahid & bilaal

hina & her eggs benedict, for being a 4'11 ray of sunshine
these past seven years & suffering through Paris with me and
her sad little macaron.

my humera for letting me sleep on her bed and being a
pretty-wonderful human being, who I pray is never tainted
by the fitnah of the dunya. she needs to relax sometimes
though.

& our bride zoya, a generous soul. who wants to paint
sunsets and loves tiny things & who is more

than deserving of the most beautiful marriage story Allah wrote for her.

aisha & fariha – my little imams for fact-checking my poems. i couldn't have published without these perfect people.

my namra for staying up with me on that wednesday night until I finished illustrating my cover. also for every late night we've stayed awake talking about life in the years before.

& our maryam. for that night we played cards and laughed and drank tea in the ugliest mugs, to obsessing over that opening line on page 3 with me.

my beautiful sobia. from the moment you supported my dream of being a spy or a painter or a writer or a vet, to the 'promise in the air' drives to the city lights - after every breakdown we've had together.

out of the entire planet, home is with you.

and finally,
thanks to little sabiha -
for staying.

Printed in Great Britain
by Amazon